AMERICA'S NATURAL WONDERS

Strange Forests, Mysterious Caverns
and Amazing Formations

By C. B. COLBY

COWARD-McCANN, Inc.   NEW YORK

Contents

PHOTO CREDITS

National Park Concessions, Inc., photo by W. Ray Scott: p. 1; New Mexico State Tourist Bureau: pp. 8, 9, 11, 16; Texas Highway Department: p. 17; Washington State Parks and Recreation Commission: p. 20; Oregon State Highway Commission: p. 36; Arkansas Publicity and Parks Commission: pp. 39, 46, 47; New Hampshire Recreation Division photo by Charles Trask: p. 48. All other photos courtesy of the National Park Service of the United States Department of the Interior. Cover photograph in Eastman Ektachrome.

Wonder-Full America!

America is truly a wonder-filled country, where around almost any bend in any road a new natural wonder may confront you.

What constitutes a "natural wonder" is often just a matter of personal opinion, and if some of my selections for this book start a controversy I'll be tickled, for in that way perhaps you will be stirred to go and take a second and closer look at some of *your* ideas of natural wonders close to home.

Often a familiar sight to one person will be a wonder to another. I well remember some years ago driving a native of Germany down the Storm King Highway along the Hudson River close to my home. To me it was just a means of getting home, for I often travel it. To this visitor it was a breath-taking drive and he asked in amazement why Americans traveled thousands of miles to see his native river Rhine when they had this far more beautiful river right in their homeland. Again, just a matter of familiarity —and personal opinion.

You who live in the West amid wide vistas, breath-taking canyons and lofty peaks, may find them too familiar for a second look, so you will enjoy the pages of scenes from the East. Those of you from the East may skip over these pages and head West to see the very canyons and mountains our western friends have skipped over. Perhaps this book will start you both across the continent to visit each other's wonders, and that will be good, for there is much in America to look at, talk about and be mighty proud of. A small part of that vast and exciting "much" appears on the following pages.

Many of the all-too-familiar natural wonders, such as Niagara Falls, are missing, but in exchange you may find some you have never heard about. Perhaps they will whet your interest in heading their way to see for yourself. That too will be good.

The material for this book came from many parts of our land and I must thank the personnel of many agencies who collected many of these photos of the places I have not as yet seen for myself.

In particular I must thank my friends, Mr. Herbert Evison, Chief of Information of the National Park Service of the United States Department of the Interior, and his able assistant, Mr. Ralph Anderson, whose friendship I have imposed upon in the past, but who seem to be still as enthusiastically co-operative as ever, which is typical of the personnel of the Park Service.

And I must thank my wife, who has camped with me in many places, for suggesting that I do this book.

I hope turning the pages ahead will start the wheels turning to get you on the high road to see as many of these sights as you can for yourself, or others more intriguing.

Matter of fact, I think I'll start out again myself. . . .

C. B. COLBY

"Nonnozoshi," the Rainbow Bridge

One of the wonders, not only of America, but of the world, is the great stone bridge known by the Indians as "Nonnozoshi," and by the white men, since its discovery in 1909, as Rainbow Bridge. This amazingly symmetrical carving by nature is located in southeastern Utah. The ages required to carve it stagger the imagination. High enough to straddle the Capitol building in Washington, it has a span of 278 feet, and its arch is as thick at the top as a three-story building (42 feet) and wide enough to accommodate an average highway. The width of the top is nearly 35 feet, and if you look closely at the photo above you will see five people standing upon the graceful arch.

Rainbow Bridge, which also appears on the cover of this book, is made of sandstone and is predominantly salmon pink in color, with streaks of brown from iron oxide running down the sides of the formation. How it came to be formed is shown in the little drawings on the opposite page. The current of an ancient river carried stones and sand against the face of the "neck" between two bends in the river, eventually wearing it through. Through the following ages, water, wind and weather wore the opening bigger and bigger until we see it as we do today, with a small stream meandering through the canyon, far below its original bed when the arch was first formed.

On August 14, 1909, Rainbow Bridge was first seen by white men—Dr. Byron Cummings, then Dean of Arts and Sciences for the University of Utah, and W. B. Douglas, a government surveyor, who had joined forces to track down rumors of such a bridge they had heard from the Indians.

ANCIENT STREAM

MODERN STREAM

Great White Throne

In the southwest corner of Utah lies Zion National Park. One of the most popular natural wonders of this wild section of our country is the Great White Throne. This giant white thrusting rock formation rises hundreds of feet above the floor of Zion Canyon. At one point the canyon is only 50 feet wide but 2,000 feet deep! This view of the Great White Throne is from near Scout's Lookout.

...ders, and one of the most famous is this
...n as Cleopatra's Needle, in Todilto Park,
...s slender spire is one of many unusual
...e. It changes color with the weather and
...ty, each change seemingly more unusual

Our Only Recently Active Volcano

Mount Lassen, one of the Cascade range of mountains in California, is the only recently active volcano in the United States, and is now a National Park known as Lassen Volcanic National Park. This peak rises 10,453 feet above sea level and is surrounded by broken rock from its own peak and cliffs. It became active again in May 1914 and continued to erupt until 1917, devastating much of the surrounding area. On May 22, 1914, a terrific blast of hot air belched from the summit with such force that it leveled trees by the thousands on Raker Peak, more than three miles away. (There are still hot springs, steam and sulphurous vents all about the area.) At one time vapor and ash rose above the crater in a column five miles high, but since 1917 the volcano has been quiet.

Carlsbad Caverns

Everyone with a bit of explorer's and adventurer's blood in his (or her) veins loves a cave, even a small one, but in Carlsbad Caverns National Park, New Mexico, in the Carlsbad Caverns, you will find more than just a cave. There are breath-taking beauty, mystery, modern conveniences and historical importance all in one. No one knows just who first discovered Carlsbad Caverns. Indians used to camp near the opening, pioneer trails passed nearby, Spanish conquistadors passing near may have entered it, and the first express trail to the West—the Butterfield Express Trail—ran close by. Formed by the solution of limestone in natural seepage over millions of years, the great rooms were hollowed out and the corridors washed out of the depths by this water seeping in from above. There are rooms with ceilings as high as 285 feet, and many miles of corridors and underground trails. Millions of bats dwell in one portion of the cave, making nightly flights outside for insects—a spectacular sight. Some passages as deep as 1,100 feet have been explored and there are many still unexplored sections even deeper. Over 37 miles of the caverns have been explored to date. The opposite page shows a section of the Hall of Giants.

Cleopatra's Needle

New Mexico is noted for its natural wond precariously balanced rock formation know north of Gallup. Hundreds of feet tall, th natural formations in this section of the sta sun, and is an object of ever-changing bea than the last.

Shiprock, "Great Winged Bird"

In the same general area as the formation known as Cleopatra's Needle, is an even more awe-inspiring formation known as Shiprock. This vast formation towering out of the plains of northwestern New Mexico was believed by the Navahos to have been a "great winged bird" which brought their ancestors to this land. Look at its towering peaks and spires. It is small wonder that the Navahos regarded it with awe and respect, for its majesty is undeniable, even to the modern-day white man.

Devil's Tower Mystery

One of the most baffling geological mysteries of all times is Devil's Tower in the northeast corner of Wyoming. This amazing tower of rock rises 865 feet high above the hilltop base on which it apparently rests. Its top—roughly an acre and a half in area—is 5,117 feet above sea level and 1,280 feet above the river bed close by. Some think that it was once solidified lava in the throat of a volcano that has been eroded away from around its rock core. Others think it to be a sheet, or "sill," of molten rock forced between rock layers. No one knows for sure just how it was formed. The Sioux Indians called it "Matéo Tepee," which meant "Grizzly Bears' Lodge." The top is covered with mosses, shrubs, ferns, grasses and sagebrush. Mice, packrats and chipmunks live there, but how they got there is another part of the mystery of Devil's Tower. It is now a National Monument.

Our Only Recently Active Volcano

Mount Lassen, one of the Cascade range of mountains in California, is the only recently active volcano in the United States, and is now a National Park known as Lassen Volcanic National Park. This peak rises 10,453 feet above sea level and is surrounded by broken rock from its own peak and cliffs. It became active again in May 1914 and continued to erupt until 1917, devastating much of the surrounding area. On May 22, 1914, a terrific blast of hot air belched from the summit with such force that it leveled trees by the thousands on Raker Peak, more than three miles away. (There are still hot springs, steam and sulphurous vents all about the area.) At one time vapor and ash rose above the crater in a column five miles high, but since 1917 the volcano has been quiet.

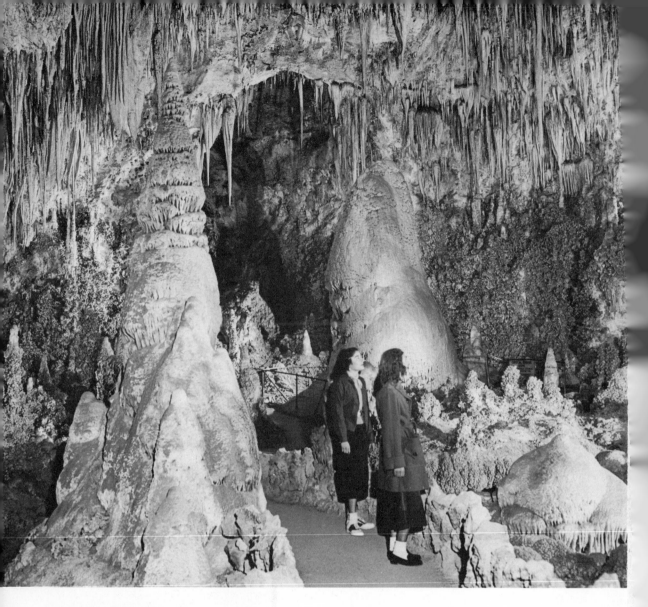

Carlsbad Caverns

Everyone with a bit of explorer's and adventurer's blood in his (or her) veins loves a cave, even a small one, but in Carlsbad Caverns National Park, New Mexico, in the Carlsbad Caverns, you will find more than just a cave. There are breath-taking beauty, mystery, modern conveniences and historical importance all in one. No one knows just who first discovered Carlsbad Caverns. Indians used to camp near the opening, pioneer trails passed nearby, Spanish conquistadors passing near may have entered it, and the first express trail to the West—the Butterfield Express Trail—ran close by. Formed by the solution of limestone in natural seepage over millions of years, the great rooms were hollowed out and the corridors washed out of the depths by this water seeping in from above. There are rooms with ceilings as high as 285 feet, and many miles of corridors and underground trails. Millions of bats dwell in one portion of the cave, making nightly flights outside for insects—a spectacular sight. Some passages as deep as 1,100 feet have been explored and there are many still unexplored sections even deeper. Over 37 miles of the caverns have been explored to date. The opposite page shows a section of the Hall of Giants.

Cleopatra's Needle

New Mexico is noted for its natural wonders, and one of the most famous is this precariously balanced rock formation known as Cleopatra's Needle, in Todilto Park, north of Gallup. Hundreds of feet tall, this slender spire is one of many unusual natural formations in this section of the state. It changes color with the weather and sun, and is an object of ever-changing beauty, each change seemingly more unusual than the last.

Shiprock, "Great Winged Bird"

In the same general area as the formation known as Cleopatra's Needle, is an even more awe-inspiring formation known as Shiprock. This vast formation towering out of the plains of northwestern New Mexico was believed by the Navahos to have been a "great winged bird" which brought their ancestors to this land. Look at its towering peaks and spires. It is small wonder that the Navahos regarded it with awe and respect, for its majesty is undeniable, even to the modern-day white man.

Devil's Tower Mystery

One of the most baffling geological mysteries of all times is Devil's Tower in the northeast corner of Wyoming. This amazing tower of rock rises 865 feet high above the hilltop base on which it apparently rests. Its top—roughly an acre and a half in area—is 5,117 feet above sea level and 1,280 feet above the river bed close by. Some think that it was once solidified lava in the throat of a volcano that has been eroded away from around its rock core. Others think it to be a sheet, or "sill," of molten rock forced between rock layers. No one knows for sure just how it was formed. The Sioux Indians called it "Matéo Tepee," which meant "Grizzly Bears' Lodge." The top is covered with mosses, shrubs, ferns, grasses and sagebrush. Mice, packrats and chipmunks live there, but how they got there is another part of the mystery of Devil's Tower. It is now a National Monument.

The Olympic Rain Forests

In the northwest corner of the United States there is an unusual area, truly a natural wonder compared with the rest of the country—the rain forests of Olympic National Park. Here, where the Quinault, Queets and Hoh rivers wend their way to the Pacific, there is more rain and moisture than any other place on the continent. Over 140 inches of rain fall in a single year, and to this is added the moisture of brooks, rivers and the nearby ocean, resulting in a fantastic jungle of moss and other moisture-loving growth. The giant Douglas fir and western red cedars are thickly festooned with layer upon layer of moss of many types, while thick ferns and still more moss thickly carpet the rain forest floor. Many delicate flowers mingle with the lush growth. The whole forest seems to be filled with a mysterious pale-green light.

"White Sands" Aren't at All!

One of our natural wonders, in direct contrast to the rain forests of the Northwest, is the White Sands *National Monument* in New Mexico. Here, stretching across 176,000 acres is a vast desert of "sand" that really isn't sand at all, but almost pure gypsum, or hydrous calcium sulphate. This material resembles sand and forms huge dunes and waves and ridges across this vast area, like a great expanse of snowdrifts. Even the animals who live in the region have changed to match its color. The mice and lizards are either white or pale in coloring to better help them escape detection in this vast gypsum desert, while those of the same species in nearby mountains are dark to match their own habitat. As the wind-blown "sand" seeks to cover the desert plants they grow taller to keep above it, and as the "sand" passes, leaving them exposed, they are often found with stems over 40 feet long, telling of the race with death they have won by growing tall.

Texas Lighthouse

About 30 miles south of Amarillo, Texas, in Palo Duro Canyon, stands the Lighthouse. This interesting formation reveals just how much erosion has taken place in the last 90 million years or longer, for the top of this high tower was once the surface of that part of Texas. Since that time, wind, weather and water have washed away the soil—all but this hard section, left to stand like a man-made tower of stone, left behind by the march of the ages. This great formation is called the Lighthouse, not only because of its shape, but because it changes color as many as 30 times during a single day. As the sun moves across the sky the towering formation seems to change in hue from reddish to gray to purple and blue and back again — a never-ending source of beauty and interest. Beyond is another erosion-caused formation.

The Grand Canyon

Above and on the opposite page are two views of one of the world's greatest natural wonders, the Grand Canyon of the Colorado River. There are so many sensational photos of this titanic Arizona gorge that it seems unfair to present only two. But perhaps these will serve to whet your interest in going out to see this great wonder yourself. Above is a view of the canyon from the South Rim near El Tovar Hotel, and on the opposite page is a view of Bright Angel Canyon from the Yavapai Museum. If you will look closely at the lower right-hand corner of the opposite photo, where the Colorado River is visible deep in the gorge, you can see the Kaibab Suspension Bridge and its shadow crossing the river. The Grand Canyon is 217 miles long and varies in width from 4 miles to nearly 20 in some spots. The Colorado River, which cut this gigantic gorge, is the second longest river in the United States (nearly 2,000 miles long) and past any given point it carries nearly a half-million tons of suspended silt every 24 hours. From the bed of the river in the gorge's depths, rims and towers rise upward over a mile, each of a different shape and color, ever changing as the day goes by.

Dry Falls, a Titanic Relic

One of the world's greatest wonders is no longer in existence, but its "skeleton" is still standing for all to marvel at. It is the site of the greatest waterfall ever to be found on the globe, and it is here in the United States, in the state of Washington. Now known as Dry Falls, this titanic relic is one of our greatest natural wonders, even though only a hint of its prehistoric grandeur is evident today. More than 15 million years ago lava welled up from beneath the surface of the earth to spread over much of the central part of the state of Washington. This lava, thousands of feet thick in places, forced the Columbia River to change its course so that it flowed around the edges of this vast lava plateau. As the lava cooled and settled and vast glaciers moved down from the north, the Columbia was dammed so that its waters took a shorter route across the lava plateau to the south. In doing so it cut great falls in the lava, to form the world's largest cataract. This stupendous falls was three miles across and more than 400 feet high! Niagara, by puny comparison, is (including Goat Island) only a mile wide and 165 feet high. There would have been room for 21 United States Capitol buildings side by side across the cataract's face, and the rim of the falls would have been more than 100 feet above the tops of the 21 buildings! Later, when the glaciers melted back to the north, the dammed Columbia was released to again flow in its old channel and the great cataract dried up, leaving this vast falls dry. On the opposite page the four stages in the development of this great wonder are shown in simplified sketches.

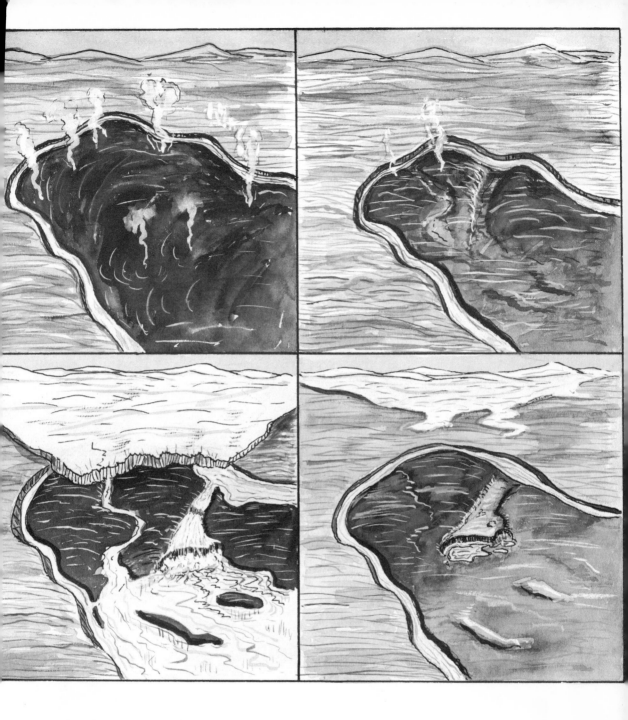

How Dry Falls Came to Be

Top left: Lava flow forces Columbia River to make channel around the northern edge of the lava plateau in central Washington State.

Top right: Underground movements form folds and depressions in vast lava plateau, while Columbia River digs its channel deeper about plateau's edge.

Lower left: Vast glaciers from the north creep down to dam Columbia River, form huge lake and force Columbia to cross lava plateau, forming giant falls.

Lower right: Glaciers melt back to north, permitting Columbia to once more use old channel, leaving great falls to become dry as shown, with only the huge cliff and lakes below it remaining, as shown in photo on opposite page.

Two Natural Wonders at a Time

Yellowstone National Park is known the world over for its geysers and hot springs. Its herd of buffalo (American bison) is also unique, for it is one of the few remaining groups of this typical American animal. Here the photographer has caught two types of natural wonders in one shot—the famous Giantess geyser and a group of American bison browsing about its base during the winter months. Yellowstone is one of the largest wildlife sanctuaries in the world and is the home of many interesting species, ranging from bear, deer, elk and antelope to bighorn sheep, moose and coyotes. The birds include 200 species, ranging from the smallest warbler to hawks, eagles, gulls and even pelicans.

Old Faithful Geyser

As typically American as apple pie and the bald eagle, Old Faithful geyser in Yellowstone National Park never fails to thrill and amaze the visitors with its clocklike regularity and stupendous spouting of steam and scalding water. With almost mechanical timing the giant geyser erupts nearly every hour—actually about every sixty-four minutes. It is occasionally a minute or so later or earlier, but still its regularity is such that tourists often wonder if it is not controlled by a hidden man. The giant spout of hot water and steam shoots as high as 150 feet into the air and looks as snowy white as new frost on the window, but is a lot more deadly. Spectators are carefully kept back out of range of the falling deluge, for this is boiling-hot water straight from the underground teakettle of Mother Nature.

Yosemite Falls

Yosemite Falls, one of the highest in the world and certainly one of the most spectacularly beautiful, has a total drop of 2,425 feet from its beginning to the bottom of the second plunge. The upper plunge is 1,430 feet, equivalent to nine Niagaras. The lower falls, 320 feet high, is nearly twice as high as Niagara. It is at its maximum flow in May and June when the winter snows are melting.

Half Dome

Another wonder to be found in Yosemite National Park is the great bulk of Half Dome, rising 8,852 feet into the air above Mirror Lake. This great stone monument to the power of the glaciers of long ago is shown from the floor of the Yosemite Valley. In the foreground is the Merced River which winds down the valley from Merced Lake to the east of Half Dome, through the valley below the mountain, and then on to the southwest. To the left of the photo above is the great falls of the Yosemite on the opposite page.

Lowest Point in the United States

This barren spot on our nation's map is the lowest there is. These people are standing more than 280 feet below bathers along our seashores, for here the "altitude" is measured, not in feet above sea level, as is the custom, but by the number of feet *below* sea level. This is Death Valley, where more than 500 square miles of land are below the level of the Pacific Ocean. A horrible nightmare of thirst and suffering to the pioneer traveler who attempted to cross it, Death Valley is now a National Monument where there have been as many as 351 clear days out of the 365 in a year. It is here that less than one and a half inches of rain have fallen during a year. Contrast this with the 140 inches of rain that fall during the same period in the rain forests of Washington State (page 15). Much of the water found in Death Valley is undrinkable, but in it there live fish of an unusual species. They are known as "desert sardines" and can live in either fresh or salt water, and in water that is far warmer than most fish prefer. The temperature of Death Valley has been known to reach 134 degrees in a modern shaded thermometer shelter.

Highest Point in the United States

Flying over Death Valley and looking almost due west from the lowest point in the United States, you can see the towering peak of Mount Whitney, the highest point in the United States. This great mountain in California straddles the border of Sequoia National Park, which runs up the south side of the mountain, over the peak and down the northern side. Here it is shown as it looks from Mount Langley to the southeast. Mount Langley, which also serves as a boundary marker for this park, is 14,042 feet high, while our tallest mountain, Mount Whitney, reaches 14,495.

Rainier, Mountain of 26 Glaciers

Another great American landmark of the Northwest is Mount Rainier, in Washington State. This beautiful snow-capped peak is only 87 feet less in height than Mount McKinley, Alaska's highest peak (20,300) yet it does not need those few feet more to be famous, and worthy of inclusion in this book. Down its sides streams the greatest single-peak glacial system in the United States. Its 26 glaciers cover 40 square miles and 12 of them are major in size and importance. The largest is Emmons Glacier, shown on the opposite page. Mount Rainier towers 14,408 feet above sea level and has a top approximately one mile square. Once an active volcano, the hollow of the peak of Mount Rainier still contains steam vents which melt the perpetual snows and form small heated caves where climbers have frequently taken refuge when caught on the peak overnight.

America's Largest Glacier

This titanic meandering river of ice, the Emmons Glacier, is the largest in the United States. It flows northeast down the rugged slopes of Mount Rainier for over five miles to a point well below the timberline at an elevation of over 4,000 feet. Such glaciers travel at the rate of about 25 feet a month, but this glacier is also moving "backwards" at the rate of about 75 feet a year. This means that the melting lower edge of the Emmons Glacier is retreating back up the slope by about 75 feet each year, due to the fact that the lower ice is melting faster than the replenishing ice moves down from above. This "two-way movement" has been going on for the past twenty years, continually exposing new ground for the first time in history. This new ground is slowly being covered with vegetation as the great ice river slowly retreats back up the mountain which spawns it.

Minerva Terrace

One of the most interesting of our natural wonders is the hot spring. This unusual natural Turkish bath is caused by hot water from deep within the earth bubbling and boiling to the surface, bringing with it quantities of mineral deposits which form weird and wonderful bowls, rims, terraces and basins about the opening of the spring. In Yellowstone National Park, where many of these natural hot springs are found, one of the most fantastic is Minerva Terrace, shown here. The many-hued terraces and basins of this great hot spring are colored by living organisms which somehow or other seem to live in the boiling temperatures of the spring. These microscopic forms of plant life, bacterial life and even one-celled creatures called diatoms thrive in the boiling temperatures of the water and steam, their bodies coloring the terraces with reds, bluish grays, browns and pinks. They too might be called a natural wonder of America.

Trees That Used to Be

The greatest and most colorful concentration of petrified wood in the world is to be found in the Petrified Forest National Monument, in Arizona. Here you may see pieces of huge tree trunks, logs and broken fragments of trunks and branches turned to stone—but what stone! These petrified logs and tree fragments from 150 million years ago are almost every color of the rainbow, and of such hardness that they will scratch all but the hardest steel. Their cracks and crevices are filled with crystals of quartz in a riot of color—amethyst, amber, green, black and flaming reds. These trees, resembling pines of South America and Australia, were swept into a prehistoric river millions of years ago and buried in sand and mud and finally volcanic ash. Through the ages the wood of the huge trees eventually turned to stone and in modern times wind and erosion uncovered these amazing relics for our admiration and wonderment.

Black Canyon of Perpetual Twilight

The Black Canyon of the Gunnison National Monument, in Colorado, is not only named for the color of the terrifying cliffs which wall it in, but for the fact that only at high noon can the sun reach to the bottom of its cleft through the plains. The walls of this great canyon are in some places more than 2,400 feet high, tapering down to a narrow slit less than 40 feet wide at the bottom, where the Gunnison River continues to cut still deeper on its way to the ocean. Many of the trees along the rim of this gloomy canyon are patriarchs. One group of piñon pines contains some veterans nearly a thousand years old. While a pigmy compared with the Grand Canyon of the Colorado, Black Canyon, with its unique cliffs of dark schists mixed with granite which has been darkened and stained by the ages, presents a mysterious and awesome sight to those who look into its twilight depths.

Florida Everglades

Looking at this vast "sea" of swampland, you may find it hard to believe that it is a National Park, yet the Everglades National Park contains one of the most interesting natural wonders of our land. Here are set aside over 1,228,500 acres of swampy jungle where nature remains in the primitive state it has been in for thousands of years. I say thousands, rather than millions, of years, for geologists say it "recently" emerged from the ocean. There is hardly a place in the Everglades more than eight feet above low tide, and a change in altitude of as little as six inches may cause a complete change in plant growth in this wonderful "new" section of our country. It contains palms, mahogany, figs, mangroves and many other tropical and semitropical trees. There are millions of wild birds, and such animals as bears, panthers, bobcats and alligators. Even the rare American crocodile lives here. The photo shows the East River Rookery, white with nesting birds—one of the sights to startle the visitor to this wild yet intriguing swampy wonder of America.

Double Wonder

Of all the many natural bridges scattered about our great land, one of the most astonishing is the vast Double Arch, to be found in Arches National Monument, in Utah. This section of Utah, not too far from the old frontier town of Moab, settled by the Mormon pioneers, is made of tan- and buff-colored sandstone. Into this soft stone nature has blown, cut, split and washed the greatest collection of bridges, arches, windows and openings in all the world. So far, 88 openings sufficiently large to be called arches have been located in the area, but there may be many more yet to be discovered. Note the people in the foreground as a comparison for size, even though they are much nearer than the arch itself.

Drilling for Dinosaurs

More than a hundred million years ago, a vast section of the country, including parts of Colorado and Utah, was a semitropical plain, populated with titanic monsters of assorted shapes and species. Suddenly death struck large numbers of these great creatures and dropped them in their tracks. Volcanic ash and other material covered them, and there they rested until 1892, when they were first reported protruding from cliffs and ledges in what is now Dinosaur National Monument. Undoubtedly the aboriginal Indians had seen them long ago and marveled at them. Many perfect skeletons have been removed by musums but great numbers still remain. The photo shows experts drilling away the face of a cliff to expose more of these long-buried giants. In all, over 300 square miles are now included in Dinosaur National Monument, but most of the reptilian relics are concentrated in the 80 acres of the original "mine" area in northeastern Utah. *Dinosaur* is derived from the Greek words *dinos* (terrible) and *saurus* (lizard).

Crater Lake

Thousands of years ago a great volcano more than 12,000 feet high towered over the state of Oregon. Not quite so long ago there was a terrific explosion, a blast so tremendous that the entire top of the mountain—estimated at more than seventeen cubic miles—was either blown off or collapsed into the crater. This formed a vast basin which eventually filled with water and is now the natural wonder known as Crater Lake. About twenty square miles in area it is six miles across and has about twenty miles of shoreline. It is just four feet less than 2,000 feet deep, making it the second deepest lake on the North American continent and the seventh deepest in the world. The water is fantastically blue and so sheltered that it is almost always mirror calm, as shown in the photo. One pointed bit of land juts from the depths on the western side of the lake. This is known as Wizard Island. Although Crater Lake is said to have been known to the Indians long ago, it was first seen by white men in 1853, when John Wesley Hillman, a young prospector looking for a rumored lost mine, discovered it.

The Grand Teton

One of the most scenic sections of our country is located in the Grand Teton National Park, in Wyoming. The scenery is practically all "vertical" here where the Teton Mountains rise above the plains of Jackson Hole. This central peak, known as the Grand Teton, rises more than 7,000 feet above the valley, and has been the backdrop for many exciting scenes from the drama of our country's history. It was first discovered in 1807-08 by John Colton of the Lewis and Clark Expedition, and from that time on this area—Jackson Hole and the Grand Teton—served as a highway and signpost for such pioneers as Jim Bridger, William Sublette, David E. Jackson (after whom the Jackson Hole area was named) and others to follow. The first settlers entered the section in 1884. Now it is one of our greatest scenic areas, open to all.

"Makosica," the Badlands

If you never get a chance to visit the moon, you can see the same kind of scenery right here in the United States. A visit to the Badlands National Monument, in the Black Hills of South Dakota, will do just as well. Here you will see weird and ever-changing views of fantastic peaks remaining from the days when volcanic cinders piled high over this area. Little by little through the ages these piles of cinders have eroded away, forming sharp "moonscape" scenery, full of peaks and towers. The cinders are still washing away bit by bit. The Dakota Indians, who called this area "Makosica" (bad lands), shunned it as a place of little water and almost no animal life, but once it teemed with creatures as weird as the mountain peaks in which they lived—the three-toed horse, the camel, rhinoceros, saber-toothed tiger and others. Many of these animals starved to death as the land changed from a fertile region to one of heat and dryness. Now it looks like a scene from the moon, or perhaps Mars, and it is much easier to visit.

America's Only Diamond Mine

Whenever you think of diamond mines you think of Africa, but oddly enough there is a diamond mine right here in the United States. Out in Arkansas, near Murfreesboro in Pike County, is what is called the Crater of Diamonds. Several thousand diamonds have been taken from this unusual natural wonder. Even though this diamond-mining area has never been important to the diamond markets of the world, it is completely unique in this part of the globe. Diamonds are usually found in yellowish clay and rock in the "roots" of prehistoric volcanos, where the great heat and pressure required for their formation was present ages ago. Here in Murfreesboro a similar small area was found, but of a bluish color. It yielded small but perfect diamonds for many years. Visitors often poke around the old buildings and the adjacent area in the hopes they may find one that everyone else has missed.

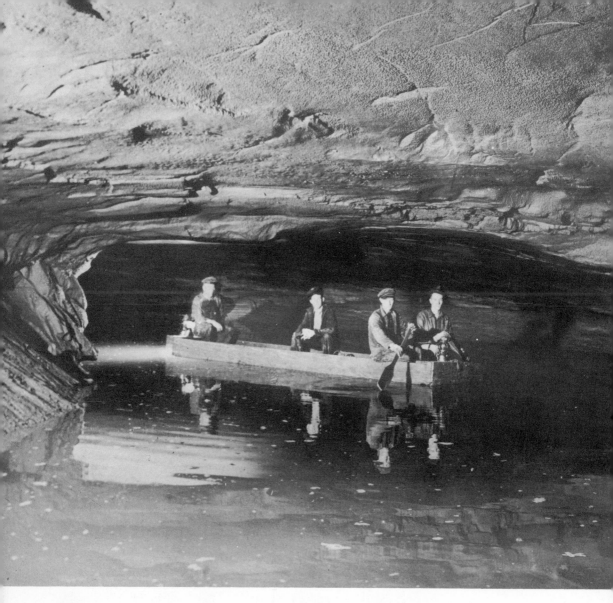

Mammoth Cave's Echo River

Often a simple action will have surprising results. Many years ago a hunter in central Kentucky wounded a bear who crawled into a cave. The hunter followed him and as a result discovered Mammoth Cave, one of the greatest underground wonders of the world. According to experts, there are at least 100,000 miles of underground passages beneath Kentucky, with a majority of them unexplored or even undiscovered, with the exception of Mammoth and its famous Echo River. There are five separate levels to this system of caverns, and Echo River flows along at its lowest, more than 360 feet below daylight. It eventually empties into the Green River, which flows through this area on the surface. Boating on Echo River is a weird and even frightening experience. Voices echo and re-echo back and forth in an amazing chorus which is almost musical. And no one has really experienced darkness until all lights have been extinguished while drifting down this river. It is then that you understand why the fish who live in its waters have no eyes, for there is absolutely nothing for them to see. The opposite page shows a formation known as the Theater Curtain in one of the cave's great rooms.

World's Greatest Glacial Pothole

Not all of the natural wonders of America are gigantic, and not all of them are hidden away in our vast West. An interesting small wonder may be found in Pennsylvania, near Archbald in Lackawanna County. Here, high on a ridge, is found the world's largest glacial pothole. Usually potholes are found in the beds of rivers and streams, where they are formed by rocks churning about with the current and wearing deep holes in the stream bottom. This great hole, over 40 feet across and 50 feet deep, was caused by rocks whirling in a stream pouring from a prehistoric glacier over 2,000 feet thick which covered this part of America. It was discovered in 1884 high on the ridge in the coal-mining area southwest of Carbondale.

Mysterious Ringing Rocks

Besides the world's largest glacial pothole, Pennsylvania has a little-publicized but mystifying natural wonder known as the Ringing Rocks. A couple of miles west of Upper Black Eddy on the Delaware River are four and a half acres of broken pock-marked red rocks which ring mysteriously when struck with a hammer or thrown onto the huge pile. In 1890 a Dr. Ott of Pleasant Valley assembled a musical scale of these stones and gave a concert accompanied by the Pleasant Valley Brass Band. These jagged stones differ from others in the area and no one knows where they came from or how they became so pock-marked and broken into these jagged pieces. For size, note leaf in cavity of rock in close-up. Some rocks are as big as footballs, others weigh many tons, but all are exceptionally heavy for their size.

Red Rocks Standing Like Men

This unusual formation was called "unka-timpe-wa-wince-pock-ich" by the Paiutes. This meant "red rocks standing like men in a bowl-shaped canyon," which is just about as close as you can get to describing Bryce Canyon. In this small area of Utah, three miles long and two miles wide, erosion has worn down into the pink and white limy sandstone to a depth of a thousand feet. What is left is a confusion of towering red, pink, white and cream-colored arches, minarets and towers.

Big-Bend Canyon Cliffs

One of our newest National Parks is Big Bend, a 700,000-acre section of spectacular scenery along the Texas border where the Rio Grande makes its famous "big bend." Here the scenery is more Mexican than American, and even the flowers, birds and animals seem to be different. Rare birds such as the Colima warbler and Aplomado falcon are found here, and the list of animals includes the Mexican black bear and the javelina. The plants too are unusual, including the rare and strange drooping juniper, the Palmer cottonwood, known only in this part of the country, and the agave, which in a spectacular display after many years of being dormant, grows to maturity almost overnight, blooms, goes to seed and dies. That this area with its forbidding and breath-taking canyons—there are three of them within the Park area— was once inhabited by prehistoric tribes of Indians is proven by finds of baskets, sandals, burned stones and other artifacts in high and dry caves along the cliffs and canyon walls.

Indian House Rock

Every state has its own natural wonders, perhaps not a Grand Canyon or an Old Faithful geyser, but nevertheless well worth visiting. Arkansas has its Buffalo River State Park, where this great cave is located. It is known as Indian House Rock and is a famous place for tourists to visit. The arched opening to this huge cave is over 75 feet across and over 25 feet high, and the "house" runs far back into the solid rock of the cliff. The photo on the opposite page was taken under the great entrance arch and shows the "chimney" hole through the roof of the cave to one side of the entrance. Note the tree growing up through this roof opening.

The Great Stone Face

Up in the author's home state of New Hampshire, high on the cliffs of Profile Mountain in Franconia Notch of the White Mountains, there is a famous profile of granite. Consisting of five layers of this rugged material—one for the chin, one for the upper lip, one for the nose, and two thinner ones for the forehead—this formation is known by three names: the Profile, the Great Stone Face, and the popular one of Old Man of the Mountains. From his lookout 1,200 feet above lovely Profile Lake the Old Man has looked down through the centuries with never a change of expression. May he look through many more with equal serenity.